TRANSGENDER LIFE™

TRANSGENDER RIGHTS AND PROTECTIONS

REBECCA T. KLEIN

ROSEN
PUBLISHING®

New York

Published in 2017 by The Rosen Publishing Group, Inc.
29 East 21st Street, New York, NY 10010

First Edition

Library of Congress Cataloging-in-Publication Data

Names: Klein, Rebecca T., author.
Title: Transgender rights and protections / Rebecca T. Klein.
Description: First Edition. | New York : Rosen Publishing, [2017] | Series: Transgender life | Audience: Grades 7–12. | Includes bibliographical references and index.
Identifiers: LCCN 2016020617| ISBN 9781499464603 (library bound) |
ISBN 9781499464580 (pbk.) | ISBN 9781499464597 (6-pack)
Subjects: LCSH: Transgender people—Juvenile literature. | Gay rights—Juvenile literature.
Classification: LCC HQ77.9 .K574 2017 | DDC 306.76/8—dc23
LC record available at https://lccn.loc.gov/2016020617

Manufactured in China

CONTENTS

INTRODUCTION

In recent years, we have seen more and more transgender people raising their voices in mainstream culture, particularly in pop culture. Critics have praised transgender actress Laverne Cox's performance on *Orange Is the New Black*. Caitlyn Jenner's reality show documents her transition and her life. There have been many opportunities to open up the conversation about transgender experiences. However, not all of those opportunities have been positive. At the same time that some cultural changes have created greater understanding and acceptance, there has also been an increase in hate crimes against transgender people—particularly transgender women of color. While the conversation has begun, these crimes let us know that we have a long way to go if we want to create a world that is safe for all people, whether or not they identify with the gender they were assigned at birth.

Whether you identify as transgender, gender nonconforming, a cisgender ally, or in a different way altogether, it is important to understand the words you will encounter when discussing transgender issues. Many of these terms may not mean what you assume they mean, and we should not make assumptions about others' gender identification. A good place to start is the word "transgender" itself.

JoAnn Brandon, mother of transgender teen Brandon Teena, whose murder was depicted in the movie *Boys Don't Cry*. Although Brandon claims elements of the movie were fictionalized, it raised awareness of violence against transgender people.

Some people use the term "trans" as shorthand for "transgender," but it originated as a prefix. As a prefix, "trans-" can mean "changing from one thing to another," as in "transform" or "transpose." It can also mean "across" or "beyond," as in "transatlantic" or "transcendence." Many of the most beautiful and powerful words and concepts in the English language begin with the prefix "trans-."

"Gender," according to the Merriam-Webster Dictionary, has two definitions: "a: SEX" and "b: the behavioral, cultural, or psychological traits typically associated with one sex." These two definitions are often the source of debate when it comes to defining the concept of gender as well as the word. People disagree about whether a person's gender is defined by their biological sex or by the behavioral, cultural, and/or psychological traits they display.

When the prefix "trans-" is attached to the word "gender," the connotations are powerful. The word means much more than just moving laterally (side-to-side) across, from one gender to another. While it can certainly mean that, it can also mean rising above, or transcending, the traditionally dictated ideas about gender altogether.

It is essential that we as a society continue to open up the conversation about transgender rights and visibility and to increase the safety and protection our society provides for transgender and gender nonconforming people. While increased understanding can certainly help to do this, legal protection is a necessary part of the process. This book will examine some of the legal rights already given to transgender people and will also explore the ways in which our laws need to change and grow.

CHAPTER 1

BRIDGING THE LANGUAGE GAP: WHAT IT MEANS (AND DOESN'T MEAN) TO BE TRANSGENDER

While history tells us that there have always been people who have not adhered to their prescribed roles and characteristics in the gender binary and who have, to varying degrees, acted and identified as a gender other than the one assigned to them at birth, the term "transgender" did not come into use until 1965. A doctor named John F. Oliven initially coined the term in a reference book called *Sexual Hygiene and Pathology*. It was meant to indicate the difference between gender identity and sexuality because, as Oliven wrote, "sexuality is not a primary factor in transvestism." If you set aside the outdated and inaccurate term "transvestism"

It is important to use correct terminology when discussing transgender issues. For example, the person pictured above is a transgender man: someone who was assigned female at birth, but who identifies as a man.

(which has the root word "vest," coming from the Latin vestis, meaning "to clothe"; being transgender is about much more than clothes), Oliven was correct in that gender identity is unrelated to sexual orientation. Transgender issues are often placed under the same umbrella as those of lesbian, gay, bisexual, and queer/questioning people, using the term LGBTQ. While transgender people—like people of varying sexual orientations—often share in the cause of challenging and redefining cultural norms and expectations regarding gender, it is important to understand that gender and sexuality are separate. Being transgender does not have any particular correlation with a person's sexual orientation. Just like nontransgender (called "cisgender") people, some transgender people are heterosexual, some are homosexual, some are bisexual, and some reject those categories altogether.

When discussing transgender issues, people often get tripped up by language. Some cisgender people are unsure of which pronouns to use, what terminology is acceptable, and which terms are offensive. Language, in this case, can often become the source of unintended misunderstandings and divisions. However, as much power as language has to divide, it has even more power to open new areas of conversation and new opportunities for connection. We have already discussed the word "transgender," but there is more to say, and many other words to talk about. These definitions are paraphrased from the Gay and Lesbian Alliance Against Defamation (GLAAD) website, which provides a useful guide for appropriate language use when discussing transgender rights.

"Transgender," as defined by GLAAD, is "an umbrella term for people whose gender identity and/or gender expression differs from what is typically associated with the sex they were assigned at birth." It is always an adjective, never a noun or a verb. It is offensive to refer to someone as "a transgender." Instead, say "a transgender person." Also, be careful to say transgender rather than transgendered. You wouldn't call someone "lesbianed" or "Mexicaned." Saying "transgendered" would be the same thing.

Pronouns are words that take the place of proper nouns and, in English, most of them are gendered (he, she, her, him, his, hers). The use of the wrong pronouns can make a transgender person very uncomfortable. Whenever possible, you should ask a transgender person which pronouns they prefer. Do not make assumptions based on appearance; just ask. If you are unable to ask or are uncomfortable asking, you can also listen to the way the person refers to themself, and to the pronouns used by the person's close friends and family.

There are a few other terms that are necessary to know when discussing transgender issues. These terms are also explained by GLAAD:

Transsexual is a term that originated in medical and psychological circles, and refers to people who have already had or are planning to have surgical and/or hormonal procedures to permanently alter their bodies. Transsexual is a much narrower term than transgender, and should never be used to describe someone unless that person expresses a desire to identify as transsexual. If the term is preferred, it, too, is an adjective and not a noun. A person is a transsexual man or a transsexual woman, not a transsexual.

Intersex is the adjective used to describe someone who was born with physical, hormonal, and genetic characteristics associated with both genders. This word replaces the outdated term "hermaphrodite."

Gender Dysphoria is a psychiatric term (replacing the outdated term gender identity disorder) that appears in the most recent Diagnostic and Statistical Manual of Mental Disorders (DSM). On the surface, it might seem offensive to classify gender dysphoria as a mental disorder. Homosexuality was once included in the DSM and has been removed, as the medical community no longer considers it to be a disease or disorder. However, many people in the transgender community believe it is helpful and necessary to have gender dysphoria officially

Emma Grace Koetter, a young woman from Georgia, identifies as genderqueer, someone who rejects the binary view of genders and may at different times identify as male, female, both, or neither.

designated as a medical condition because this makes a stronger case for requiring insurance companies to cover hormonal and surgical treatments.

Cisgender is a term that is sometimes used to describe people who are not transgender. It is simply shorthand for "nontransgender." A cisgender person is a person who identifies as and feels comfortable with the gender they were assigned at birth.

CROSS DRESSING, DRAG, AND GENDER NONCONFORMING

Some people have trouble recognizing and understanding the difference between being transgender and being a cross-dresser or a drag queen/king. While those three things al involve, to differing degrees, going outside of societa expectations for one's gender, there are important distinctions between the three. Drag kings and drag queens dress in often exaggerated and sometimes comedic or parodied versions o the opposite gender's clothing for the sake of entertainment Drag performers do not necessarily cross-dress when they are not performing. Cross-dressers are (often heterosexual) males who dress in clothing, makeup, and accessories that are usually marketed to and culturally associated with women. The term "transvestite" used to be synonymous with cross-dresser, but i is outdated and can be offensive, so it is a good idea to avoid it Some people cross-dress only in private, while others go out in public. Occasionally, cross-dressing can be an initial step in realizing or accepting oneself as transgender or a first step in the process of transitioning. However, there are many people both homosexual and heterosexual, who cross-dress withou desiring to live full-time as the opposite gender.

The term "gender nonconforming" refers to people (such as cross-dressers) who do not subscribe or conform to traditional ideas about the expression of masculinity or femininity. Gende nonconforming people may or may not identify as transgender. Also, not all transgender people identify as gender nonconforming. Some transgender people adhere to very traditional styles of dress and gender expression. A male-identified person who wears clothes that are culturally associated with women might identify as gender nonconforming, but not as transgender. On the other hand, a person who was assigned male at birth but feels that she is truly female and dresses according to her true gender might identify as transgender, but not as gender nonconforming.

It is important to note that transgender people feel on every level that their gender is different from the one they were assigned at birth. Being transgender goes beyond clothing and accessories, beyond external characteristics altogether.

Genderqueer is a term sometimes used by people who reject the gender binary altogether; that is, they do not identify as strictly male or female. They may see gender as a spectrum, in which they fall somewhere in between male and female, or they may identify outside of those genders altogether. Genderqueer should only be used if a person uses the term themselves, and should never be used as a synonym for transsexual or transgender.

THE TRANSITIONING PROCESS

When a person comes out as transgender and acknowledges the desire to transition, they begin a process that can take many different paths, a process that may continue indefinitely. Some people take hormones that change their external appearance but

Drag queens are men who dress up in traditionally female clothing and accessories for the sake of public entertainment. Cross-dressers might dress in the opposite gender's clothing in private or in public.

choose not to have surgery that alters their sexual organs. Some people begin with hormones and eventually do have surgery. Some do not take hormones or have surgery.

There are also different types of surgery. Choosing not to have surgery does not make a person any less transgender. It is unnecessary and can be offensive to scrutinize whether a person's transition will include sex-reassignment surgery (SRS). As GLAAD puts it, "Don't ask if a transgender person has had 'the surgery' or if they are 'pre-op' or 'post-op.' If a transgender person wants to talk to you about such matters, they will bring it up. Similarly, it wouldn't be appropriate to ask a nontransgender person about how they have sex, so the same courtesy should be extended to transgender people." In addition to being an intrusive question, terms like "pre-op" and "post-op" imply that all transgender people will eventually have surgery, which is not true. If someone chooses to keep the biological sex they were born with but to express their true gender identity, this does not make them less transgender. The bottom line is, unless the person chooses to discuss the matter openly, it is no one else's business whether a transgender person takes hormones, has surgery, does both, or does neither.

CHAPTER 2

REVOLUTION, EVOLUTION:
THE HISTORY OF THE TRANSGENDER RIGHTS MOVEMENT

While mainstream culture has only recently begun openly discussing transgender rights, there have been many people, both transgender and cisgender, fighting for equality for a long time, sometimes alongside other groups of queer people and sometimes separately. These activists have developed several events that occur every year to bring awareness to transgender causes, concerns, and achievements. These events include International Transgender Day of Visibility (TDOV), Transgender Awareness Week, Transgender Day of Remembrance, and Trans March.

A candlelight vigil in Hyderabad, India, honoring victims of anti-trans violence on the 2015 Transgender Day of Remembrance, November 20. On this day, vigils are held across the world.

EARLY TRANSGENDER RIGHTS ACTIVISTS

One of the earliest groups of transgender activists was the Cercle Hermaphroditos, a group organized in 1895 in New York by people who described themselves as "androgynes." This group's self-proclaimed purpose was "to unite for defense against the world's bitter persecution." By the 1950s and 1960s, transgender visibility had begun to increase a bit. In 1952, a woman named Christine Jorgenson became the first person to be widely publicized as having sexual reassignment surgery (male to female). Despite having had surgery, Jorgenson was denied a marriage license when she tried to marry a man, and that man lost his job when people found out about his engagement to Jorgenson.

The other famous transgender person of the time was Virginia Prince. Prince had begun living full-time as a woman in the 1940s, and in 1952 she launched *Transvestia: The Journal of the American Society for Equality in Dress*. That magazine published only two issues, but by 1960, Prince founded another magazine, also called *Transvestia*, as well as a club for cross-dressers called Hose and Heels. Prince believed that the gender binary was a harmful concept that prevented humans from realizing their full potential, and she believed that cross-dressing was one way to challenge the binary. She worked closely with famed researcher Alfred Kinsey to bring transgender causes to the attention of the social science community.

By 1966, in San Francisco, transgender politics became militant when a group of transgender prostitutes staged a riotous uprising against police harassment at a restaurant called Compton's Cafeteria, in San Francisco's Tenderloin district. By the late 1960s, transgender politics became closely associated with gay liberation, and some transgender women played an important role in sparking the historical 1969 uprising at the Stonewall Inn in New York City. By the late 1960s and early 1970s, many transgender political organizations came into being, including Street Transvestite Action Revolutionaries (STAR), founded by Sylvia Rivera (a veteran of Stonewall) and Marsha P. Johnson, and the Queens Liberation Front, jointly founded by gay drag performer and activist Lee Brewster and heterosexual cross-dresser Bunny Eisenhower. Another milestone in the late

Transgender actress and activist Laverne Cox poses with her *Orange Is the New Black* co-star, Elizabeth Rodriguez, at the 2016 Screen Actors Guild Awards.

1960s was the founding of the Labyrinth Foundation Counseling Service, the first community organization designed to serve the needs of female-to-male (FTM) transsexuals.

In the 1970s, although some progress was being made in areas such as health care and the right to change gender designation on documents issued by the state, the transgender community was beginning to experience some backlash from the gay, lesbian, and feminist communities. In the 1980s, the female-to-male transgender community began to take shape. Lou Sullivan founded an FTM support group that eventually became FTM International. During the late 1980s and early 1990s, the AIDS crisis began to bring transgender causes back onto the radar of larger social justice movements and, in 1992, activist Leslie Feinberg published *Transgender Liberation: A Movement Whose Time Has Come*. Feinberg's pamphlet ushered in a new political era for transgender people, inspiring groups such as Transgender Nation and Transexual Menace.

In 1993, transgender man Brandon Teena, along with two of his friends, was brutally murdered in Nebraska. This heinous crime brought attention to hate crimes and antitransgender violence and was portrayed in the 2000 film *Boys Don't Cry*. The late 1990s saw the launch of the website *Remembering Our Dead*, as well as the National Day of Remembrance and the group Gender Public Advocacy Coalition (Gender PAC).

TRANSGENDER RIGHTS EVENTS

As described by Trans Student Educational Resources, the Transgender Day of Visibility "aims to bring attention to the accomplishments of trans people around the globe while fighting cissexism and transphobia by spreading knowledge of the trans

Some of the thousands of participants in the 2013 Trans March in San Francisco, which began in Mission Delores Park and continued on to the Civic Center.

community." It is a day to express pride and to build awareness around transgender causes and triumphs. TDOV occurs on March 31 each year.

Transgender Awareness Week happens from November 14 to 20 each year. Like TDOV, Transgender Awareness Week seeks to raise the visibility of the transgender community, as well as to bring attention to the issues faced by transgender and gender nonconforming people. Transgender Awareness Week culminates in the Transgender Day of Remembrance.

PIONEERS OF TRANS VISIBILITY

While Caitlyn Jenner has received more media attention than many other transgender people, she is neither the first nor the only person to discuss her transition publicly and to fight for equality. There are many activists, actors, models, writers, and other famous people who identify loudly and proudly as transgender and who are making news and history. Here are a few:

Laverne Cox is one of the best-known transgender celebrities currently in the spotlight. Her performance as Sophia on the Netflix series *Orange Is the New Black* has received critical acclaim for both her acting ability and for the attention the character brings to transgender causes. Cox's role on *Orange Is the New Black* marks the first time a transgender woman of color has had a leading role on a scripted series broadcast on mainstream television. Cox has been nominated for an Emmy for her performance.

Bryanna Jenkins is the founder of the Baltimore Trans Alliance. In July 2015, the organization staged a march to protest the killing of Mia Henderson, a young transgender woman murdered in Baltimore, as well as the ten (documented) other trans women killed that year. Bryanna's work brings attention to the disproportionate rates of harassment and violence, at the hands of police and civilians, faced

Model Laith Ashley De La Cruz, who was featured in a Barney's ad campaign not long after beginning his medical transition, has been making waves on Instagram. Laverne Cox posted one of De La Cruz's photos to her Instagram account, and his popularity exploded. In November 2015, he was named *Out* magazine's "Man Crush Monday."

Jazz Jennings first came into the spotlight at the age of six, when she was interviewed by Barbara Walters. At the age of fifteen, Jazz, along with her family, launched a reality show about the daily aspects of being a teenage girl. Since then, Jazz and her family have affirmed her female gender, and she wishes to identify simply as a teenage girl, even as she brings attention to transgender causes, such as her right to use the girls' bathrooms and play on girls' sports teams.

Activist and writer Janet Mock chronicled her transition in the book *Redefining Realness*. She also hosts a show on MSNBC and has written articles for various publications. In addition to discussing her experiences as a transgender woman, Mock is a powerful voice in many other aspects of culture.

The Transgender Day of Remembrance, on November 20, is a day to remember the people who have lost their lives in acts of antitransgender violence. Gwendolyn Ann Smith, a transgender advocate, began the observance to honor Rita Hester, a transgender woman who was murdered in 1998. That first vigil honored all transgender people lost to violence that year, and the tradition has continued each year since then.

Around the United States and the world, Trans March events take place in conjunction with LGBTQ Pride celebrations each year. Designed to raise visibility for the "T" in "LGBTQ," Trans

JANET MOCK

Janet Mock is a vocal activist for many causes, including transgender rights. She tells the story of her own transition in her book *Redefining Realness*, and hosts a talk show on cable channel MSNBC.

Marches have become an important aspect of Pride celebrations in many cities. Some of the biggest Trans March events occur in San Francisco and Toronto.

Understanding the ways that our laws do and do not protect transgender people is difficult for a few different reasons. First of all, "the law" is a complicated term. In the United States, there is the Constitution (federal law), and then there are state laws. While the Constitution prohibits discrimination by the government according to gender and sexual orientation, it does not specifically mention transgender people. However, some states do have laws that specifically protect transgender people. Additionally, although the Constitution does not specifically mention transgender people, many Constitutional laws can be interpreted in such a way that they cover transgender people under another umbrella. As we discuss specific legal rights and situations, we will explore some federal laws, some state laws, and some of these interpretations of Constitutional laws. Both the laws and the interpretations are the result of the real battles for trans rights waged by past and current activists.

CHAPTER 3

GENDERED SPACES:
RIGHTS FOR TRANSGENDER PEOPLE IN PUBLIC PLACES

From the bathroom to the basketball court, our world is full of places and situations in which people are divided by gender. This can be problematic for cisgender people under certain circumstances, and it presents even more difficulty for transgender and gender nonconforming people. The good news, however, is that there are laws that prohibit gender discrimination, and it is fairly logical to argue that these laws cover transgender people as well. According to the American Civil Liberties Union (ACLU), there are several state agencies and courts (including those in Hawaii, California, Massachusetts, Connecticut, New Jersey, Vermont, and New York) that have ruled that their laws prohibiting discrimination based on sex also cover transgender people. Additionally, a few states have ruled that gender dysphoria is covered under laws that protect people from being discriminated against based on disability. This is one reason why some transgender advocates support the inclusion of gender

The right of transgender people to use public bathrooms of their choice has been hotly contested and covered in the media.

dysphoria in the DSM-5, although it might seem offensive to designate it as a disability.

Despite the states that have ruled in favor of protection for transgender people, there are many that have not issued such rulings. The word "discrimination" is very general, so putting legal protections into practice and holding organizations accountable can be more complicated than it should be. This is true of all antidiscrimination laws, but when it comes to protecting transgender people, there are even more intricacies.

BATHROOM LAWS

One public place where transgender people often face difficulty is the bathroom. It would be fairly simple for all businesses and public places to have single-user bathrooms that are not designated for any specific gender. However, not all places provide such bathrooms. Furthermore, many transgender people feel it is important to have the right to use the bathroom designated for their identified gender, regardless of whether others perceive them as that gender or not. For these reasons, there has been much debate over who should be able to use the bathrooms designated for women and men. Many people have weighed in on the bathroom controversy, giving voice to the ridiculousness of the notion that these laws could even be enforced unless someone was positioned at the entrance of bathrooms, checking birth certificates, driver's licenses, and genitals.

The bathroom debate has received a lot of recent media attention, and more and more companies and schools are changing their policies to create a more inclusive environment for transgender people. These policies can be helpful for other people, too. Many people run into trouble when there is no unisex bathroom option, like parents with children of another gender or people with disabled relatives of another gender. All of these people can benefit from laws that mandate a gender-neutral option in public bathrooms.

But some transgender activists believe that gender-neutral bathrooms are not a good solution. Lila Perry is a teen activist who has been fighting for inclusive bathroom accommodations in schools, and she believes that gender-neutral bathrooms are not an acceptable option. "I wasn't hurting anyone, and I didn't want to feel segregated out," said Perry in an interview with St.

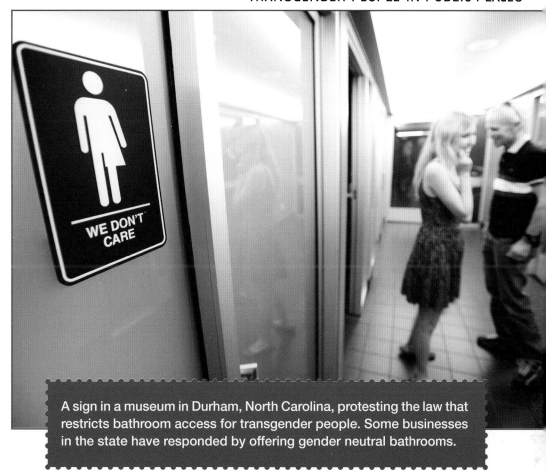

A sign in a museum in Durham, North Carolina, protesting the law that restricts bathroom access for transgender people. Some businesses in the state have responded by offering gender neutral bathrooms.

Louis television station KMOV. "I am a girl." If transgender people are not granted express legal rights to use the bathroom of their identified gender and instead are encouraged to use gender-neutral bathrooms, trans activists argue that this impedes their free gender expression.

SPORTS TEAMS

Title IX is a law that prohibits gender-based discrimination on sports teams. However, the extent to which and the ways in which this law protects transgender students varies from state to state. According to Pat Griffin writing for the National Federation of State High School Associations, "Because state policies vary, a transgender student's opportunity to participate on high school athletic teams may be determined by the state in which they live." Griffin also points out that even when schools do not blatantly prohibit transgender students from participating on teams of their identified gender, they often have policies that make this difficult and even dangerous. For instance, a school may allow a transgender boy to play on the boys' basketball team but require him to change in the girls' locker room because he was assigned female at birth. The same goes for transgender girls, who may

Laws regarding transgender people and sports are continually evolving. In many states, transgender people are allowed to compete on teams of their identified gender even if they have not undergone sex reassignment surgery.

be required to change in boys' locker rooms. Both of these situations are potentially humiliating and emotionally dangerous, and transgender girls often face serious physical danger in boys' locker rooms.

According to Griffin, many state associations are establishing policies to protect and support the inclusion of transgender students on sports teams. In order to truly protect transgender students, state laws, as well as school policies, need to evolve to the point where they take all aspects of transgender students' physical and mental well-being into consideration. Fortunately, changes are being made today not just on the local and state levels, but at the national and international levels as well. For example, the International Olympic Committee adopted guidelines in January 2006 allowing transgender athletes to compete in their gender category without first having to undergo sex reassignment surgery.

THE MICHIGAN CONTROVERSY

Bathrooms and sports teams are not the only public arenas that are divided by gender. Sometimes, communities that are supposedly fighting against discrimination end up discriminating against transgender people themselves. In 1991, for example, the Michigan Womyn's Music Festival created controversy by banning transgender women from attending and kicking out a festivalgoer named Nancy Burkholder on the assumption that she was transsexual. Third-wave feminist and transgender activist Emi Koyama maintains a question and answer page about this controversy at her website, eminism.org, detailing the policy that caused the controversy and the development of Camp Trans, an event organized in protest of the festival in 1992.

RIGHTS FOR TRANSGENDER PEOPLE IN PRISON

Prisons are another example of public spaces that are segregated by gender. Transgender people in prison are particularly vulnerable to mental and physical harassment. Often, transgender offenders are placed in prisons according to their assigned gender rather than their identified gender, regardless of how they present. According to an article in *The New York Times*, transgender people are more likely than other sectors of the population to be imprisoned in the first place and face "disproportionate risks" while they are in prison. According to the article, transgender prison inmates are also more likely to report unwanted sexual activity with other inmates or prison guards. Transgender inmates are often placed in solitary confinement, which is supposed to be for their own protection against sexual or physical assaults, although it can end up being assaultive itself. In addition to the psychological toll of isolation, solitary confinement increases the risk of assault by prison guards. Prisoners in solitary confinement are also deprived of group therapy, as well as education programs that could increase their chances of employment upon release.

Prisons also have a history of denying hormone therapy to transgender inmates, even if they have been under treatment prior to being incarcerated. In one well-known case, a transgender woman named Ashley Diamond attempted suicide after being denied hormones during her prison term. Following her release, she has become an outspoken critic of the abuse of transgender prisoners by prison officials. The denial of hormone therapy was addressed on the Netflix series *Orange Is the New Black*, when Laverne Cox's character, Sophia, was denied hormones she had previously been using.

Despite these disheartening facts, there is some progress being made. In April 2014, the Justice Department handed down a ruling that declared the denial of hormone therapy to transgender inmates unconstitutional. This means that state laws barring hormone therapy for prisoners are illegal. (Unfortunately, 44 percent of transgender prisoners still report being denied hormone treatment.) Other signs of progress include the fact that California has begun covering sexual reassignment surgery for inmates, and many facilities, including Rikers Island in New York, have begun offering alternative housing facilities for transgender women.

Pictured here is Rikers Island, a New York City prison complex where violence towards inmates by guards is common. Transgender inmates often face disproportionately violent treatment in prison.

Regarding the policy itself, Koyama says,

> Michigan Womyn's Music Festival holds the policy that only "womyn-born womyn" are allowed to enter, meaning that only those who have lived their entire lives as females can participate in the festival. Put more blatantly, the policy is intended to exclude transsexual people, whether they are male-to-female transsexuals (trans women) or female-to-male transsexuals (trans men). Many in the trans communities as well as queer and women's communities feel that this policy is oppressive, although their proposed alternatives may vary. Note that many transsexual women actually feel that they have always been women, albeit misidentification by others, and thus feel that the phrase "womyn-born womyn" should include them.

Koyama goes on to point out that although the festival bars transsexual women, it allows many other women who may identify as transgender or gender nonconforming to participate, including butch women, bearded women, and drag king performers. The Michigan Womyn's Music Festival controversy illustrates the tension that can occur between some feminist organizations and trans activists over gender identification.

In response to this discrimination, the first Camp Trans was held in 1994, across the street from the entrance to the festival. Initially, it was an event for transsexuals and their allies, but over the years it began to attract more genderqueer and radical-lesbian-feminist women, as well as transsexual women. Koyama discusses the fact that there was a lot of debate among Camp Trans participants themselves. Some believed that only postoperative transsexual women should be allowed to enter the festival, but many others argued that anyone who identifies as a woman should be able to attend, regardless of her genitals. The 2002 mission statement read: "[O]ur mission is to educate the attendees of Michigan Womyn's Music Festival about the 'womyn-born-womyn only' policy with the end goal of broadening that policy to include ALL self-identified womyn."

In bathrooms, in prisons, on the playing field, and in other public spaces, transgender people continue to fight for the right to exercise their gender expression and to occupy spaces that agree with their true genders. Although there is still a lot of work to do, laws and communities continue to evolve and move toward allowing all people to define their own gender identities and to express them in the ways they choose.

CHAPTER 4

THE RIGHT TO WELLNESS:

HEALTH CARE AND HOUSING RIGHTS FOR TRANSGENDER PEOPLE

Only in recent years have our laws and lawmakers begun to deal with transgender people's rights to health care, both mental and physical. It is important for anyone to have access to quality health care, but it can be especially important for transgender people. Transitioning can be costly if a person chooses to undergo hormone therapy or gender affirmation surgery, and it is important to receive proper medical care leading up to, during, and following hormone therapy and/or surgery.

Although we still lack national laws that explicitly protect transgender people against discrimination in health care, there are many existing laws that can be interpreted to include transgender people in their protections. The National Center for Transgender

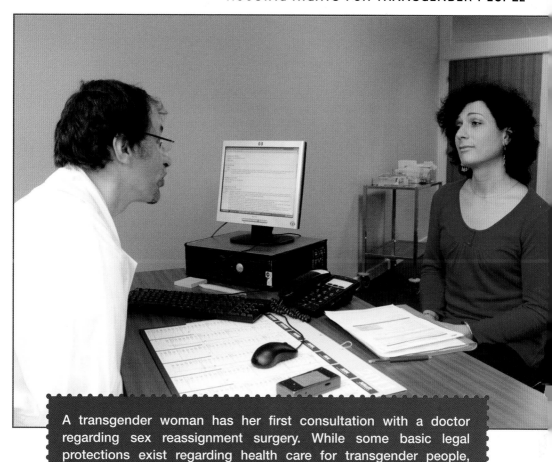

A transgender woman has her first consultation with a doctor regarding sex reassignment surgery. While some basic legal protections exist regarding health care for transgender people, specific procedures covered vary with different insurance plans.

Equality (NCTE) provides a useful guide to these laws and the ways that they benefit transgender people. The NCTE website mentions the following laws as protecting transgender people when it comes to health care:

- The Affordable Care Act prohibits sex discrimination in any federally funded health care program, and this prohibition has been interpreted to include discrimination against transgender and gender nonconforming people. It also states that transgender people cannot be denied health insurance simply for being transgender.

- The Joint Commission hospital accreditation standards state that hospitals must develop internal policies against discrimination based on sexual orientation and gender identity.
- The Health Insurance Portability and Accountability Act (HIPAA) mandates confidentiality and protects against disclosure of information that may identify an individual, including transgender status. It also mandates that patients have access to their own information.
- Medicare and Medicaid dictate that patients have the right to choose their own visitors when hospitalized. This means that hospital staff may not discriminate or deny visitation rights to transgender people.
- The Nursing Home Reform Act protects nursing home residents against abuse and mistreatment and guarantees their right to choose visitors. It also protects their right to dignity and self-determination and states that they may file grievances in the case of mistreatment.

Medical facilities and professionals that may not discriminate against transgender people include doctors' offices, hospital emergency rooms, home health care providers, drug rehab programs, nursing homes, community health clinics, and medical care facilities in prison. Medical professionals must address a transgender person by their preferred name and pronouns, regardless of whether or not the person has obtained a legal name change or taken any medical steps in transitioning. The following types of discrimination are also prohibited:

- Refusal of admission;
- Unnecessary, intrusive examinations;
- Refusal to provide restroom access consistent with gender identity;
- Any type of harassment, intimidation, or coercion;

- Mandating "conversion therapy" to change one's gender identity;
- Refusal to provide medical advocacy, counseling, or other support services;
- Refusal to provide health insurance simply because a person is transgender.

In addition to physical health, mental health can also be a concern for transgender people, just as it can be for cisgender people. Sometimes it is an even greater concern because of the discrimination and difficulty transgender people may face during and after transitioning. Some doctors may also require psychological therapy before prescribing hormone therapy to

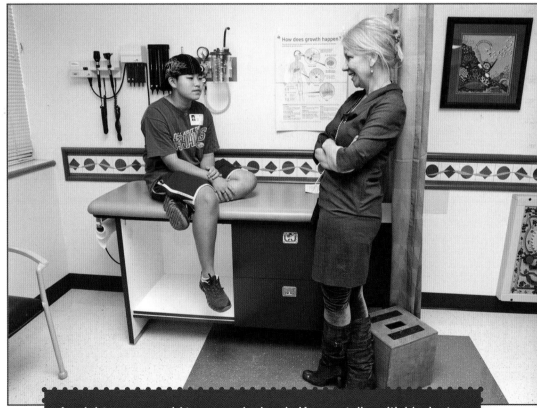

An eighteen-year-old transgender boy in Kansas talks with his doctor. Doctors may require psychological therapy before they will allow transgender patients to begin hormone therapy.

patients. In some states, including New York, if mental health care is covered by an insurance provider, that provider is required to cover treatment for gender dysphoria, including hormone therapy and some types of surgery.

Transgender people who experience discrimination in a health care setting have several options for filing complaints. In New York State, for instance, complaints of discrimination in a medical facility may be filed with the New York State Department of Health, the New York State Division of Human Rights, the attorney general, or the New York City Commission on Human Rights if they are in New York City. The Joint Commission, an independent body that investigates and accredits hospitals, has a policy of nondiscrimination, and complaints may also be filed with that organization.

EMERGENCY ROOM HORROR STORY

One person's story, detailed in the *Journal of Emergency Nursing*, clearly illustrates the discrimination transgender people can face in medical settings. The article's title alone, "I Was a Spectacle...A Freak Show At A Circus: One Transgender Person's ED [Emergency Department] Experience and Implications For Nursing Practice," speaks volumes to the ways that medical staff can negatively impact transgender people. In the article,

Brandon James describes the humiliation he was subjected to by staff members in an unspecified emergency department in the southeastern United States. James was assigned female at birth, but identifies and presents as male. However, his driver's license and electronic medical records identified him as female. The admissions staff at the emergency department's check-in desk seemed confused by this discrepancy and handled it in a very unprofessional manner.

According to James, "They come up and she's like, 'That's a girl.' Pointing at me saying, 'No, that's really a girl.' It wasn't business-like at all. I was a spectacle. I was a freak show at the circus." Thankfully, the nurse that James saw after this negative experience was much more understanding: "She was awesome because she was matter-of-fact. She was concerned with my care. That [being transgender] didn't matter to her. What mattered was making sure I was physically OK. That was very reassuring." However, when he was directed back to the check-in desk, Brandon faced further humiliation as another staff member refused to acknowledge him as a man and repeatedly referred to him as "Ms. James."

James's experience illustrates the necessity of laws and policies that protect transgender people in medical settings. Medical professionals are in the position to affect whether or not a person feels comfortable seeking care and to make that care either more or less accessible to the person. The upside of this article is that James's experience was used to convince nursing professionals how important it is to treat transgender people with dignity. The article's authors, both nursing professionals, advocate for education and awareness among medical professionals in all positions and policies that lead to greater access to health care for transgender patients

HOUSING AND EMPLOYMENT DISCRIMINATION

Housing and employment are two other areas in which there are not yet many laws on the books specifically protecting transgender people. However, just as with sports teams and health care, courts have consistently ruled that the laws protecting against discrimination based on sex also can cover gender identity. This means that even where transgender people are not explicitly protected, they have some legal recourse when it comes to discrimination in housing or employment.

Title VII of the 1964 Civil Rights Act prohibits discrimination according to sex (among other characteristics) by employers who have more than fifteen employees on their payroll. Although some older court decisions denied transgender people protection under this law, more recent decisions have reversed that

Transgender people may face discrimination in housing, but this is illegal according to the Fair Housing Act, which prohibits discrimination based on gender. The US Housing Department has determined that this includes transgender people.

denial. In Washington, DC, a federal district court ruled that it is illegal under Title VII to discriminate against an employee for transitioning from one gender to another. US attorney general Eric Holder's office voiced its support for this position in 2014. Transgender people who experience employment discrimination may file complaints with the US Equal Opportunity Employment Commission, which can investigate claims, arrange mediation, broker a settlement, file a lawsuit, or give an individual permission to file their own lawsuit.

The Fair Housing Act prohibits sex discrimination in housing, and the US Department of Housing and Urban Development (HUD) has ruled that this covers gender identity and gender nonconformity. HUD also mandates that in homeless shelters where residents are segregated by gender, transgender people must be housed according to their gender identity rather than the gender they were assigned at birth. Also, all shelters receiving funding through the Violence Against Women Act are prohibited from discriminating against transgender people.

CHAPTER 5

TRANSCENDING IGNORANCE:
ANTIBULLYING AND ANTI-HATE CRIME LAWS

A hate crime is a crime that is committed deliberately against a person because they are identified with a certain group against which the attacker is biased. Hate crimes carry stricter and more severe penalties than simple assaults. According to the National Center for Transgender Equality, more than one in four transgender people has experienced an assault driven by antitransgender bias. Lambda Legal states that 44 percent of hate murders reported in 2010 were committed against transgender women.

The terror of potential attacks is compounded by the fact that transgender people are often afraid to seek the assistance of police, for fear of facing further harassment at the hands of law enforcement officials. According to Lambda Legal,

In West Hollywood, California, a transgender woman reads the life story of another trans woman who was killed in a hate crime, stressing that her life story was prematurely ended.

Police often participate in the intimidation themselves rather than providing protection; they often use abusive language, humiliate TGNC [transgender and non-conforming] people and are widely responsible for injuries during custody and on routine patrols. Twenty-two percent of the 6,450 transgender and gender-nonconforming respondents to the 2011 National Transgender Discrimination Survey (NTDS) who had interacted with police said they'd been harassed by them, with rates even higher among people of color.

Community organizer Lourdes Ashley Hunter told Lambda Legal, "The police profile transgender individuals a lot. They think that we're all sex workers. There are cases where they harass people, disrespect them and take away their humanity. Sexual assault cases are not uncommon. They also use inappropriate pronouns, offensive language and pejorative terms."

Considering the prevalence of violent attacks against transgender people—particularly transgender women of color— in recent years, it became clear that it was essential to have laws on the books that condemn harassment, violence, and hate crimes against transgender people. In 2009, the Matthew Shepard and James Byrd Jr. Hate Crimes Prevention Act officially became law.

President Barack Obama with the families of James Byrd Jr. and Matthew Shepherd, who were both killed in hate crimes, at the signing of the Hate Crimes Prevention Act into law in 2009. The law is named for Byrd and Shepherd.

Expanding on older hate-crime legislation from 1969, the new law explicitly classifies as hate crimes those that are motivated by sexual orientation, a person's actual or perceived gender, or gender identity. The act also provides funding to state and local agencies investigating hate crimes.

Official legislation is a huge triumph and a necessary step in eradicating antitransgender crimes, but it is not enough on its own. Additionally, it is essential that cisgender supporters ally themselves with their transgender friends, classmates, coworkers, and fellow humans and stand in solidarity against these attacks. Schools are excellent places for both of these processes to begin. When students learn early in life to create safe, inclusive, and supportive environments, they can help to transform society as a whole. The social norms set in schools often become the norms of offices and other workplaces once the next generation enters the workforce.

In an earlier chapter, we examined laws that affect students' usage of bathrooms and participation on sports teams, but what about the laws that govern the overall school environment? In addition to the law that prohibits violent bias crimes, are there laws that protect transgender students from discrimination and verbal or emotional harassment in the classrooms and hallways of our schools? As with all of the other laws we have discussed, the answer is "yes, but it's complicated." The law has a long way to go to provide explicit protections against harassment based on gender identity the way it protects against harassment based on race, sexual orientation, and sex. Some states, as well as some schools, provide specific protections for transgender students, while others do not. However, existing laws can certainly be used to protect transgender students even where they do not specifically mention them.

Antibullying laws have important implications for transgender students. These laws do not specify on what grounds bullying is prohibited; it is forbidden across the board. Whether or not a state has specific protections for transgender students, any physical or emotional harassment should be intolerable under antibullying policies. Many schools include gender identity in the issues discussed during bullying prevention. Whether you identify as transgender, gender nonconforming, or a trans ally, you can help to raise awareness of transgender issues and to prevent antitransgender bullying. When you hear your peers making

The fight continues for equal rights and protections for people of all gender identities. Although much progress has been made, there remains lots of work to be done!

jokes or comments that are insulting or offensive to transgender people, call them out.

The First Amendment to the Constitution protects the right to freedom of speech and expression. This right is guaranteed to all Americans, and transgender people should not be hindered from exercising this right. Although school rules and policies may vary by state, district, and individual school, those policies should not violate the Constitution. If you are a transgender student and you feel that your constitutional rights are being violated, you have every right to challenge the policy that violates them. Even if you identify as cisgender, you can personally benefit from an environment in which people are free to express their gender identity in whichever way they choose. Nobody should be required to dress, speak, or carry themselves in any particular way simply because of the gender they were assigned at birth.

HOW CISGENDER KIDS CAN BE ALLIES TO THEIR TRANSGENDER FRIENDS

The word "ally" means a person who gives help and support to another person or group. Allies do not identify as a certain race, gender, sexual orientation, or gender identity but want to support and advocate for members of that community. Cisgender people who believe that everyone should be able to express their true gender identity in whatever ways they choose can support the fight for transgender rights.

(continued on the next page)

(continued from the previous page)

There are several organizations that offer tips to cisgender people seeking to be allies. Here are a few tips recommended by PFLAG and GLAAD:

- Listen to and seek out the voices of transgender people when trying to understand transgender issues. Have conversations with transgender people you know, keeping in mind the tips for being respectful and not intrusive. Ask transgender people how they prefer to identify and what pronouns they prefer. Do not make assumptions. Listen more than you talk.

- Understand how the issue of "coming out" is different for transgender people than it is for lesbian, bisexual, or gay people. While some transgender people choose to openly identify that way for personal reasons or for the sake of activism, others simply want to live as their authentic gender, without telling people that it differs from the one they were assigned at birth. This does not make them any less courageous than the people who are vocal about their transgender status.

- Be patient as a person defines or questions their gender identity. This is not always a straightforward process. The name and pronouns by which a person identifies may change over time, more than once. There is no one process to follow for transitioning. The path toward authentic identity and expression differs for every person, and for many people it is ongoing.

- Understand that gender is complicated for everyone. Many people never even think to question their gender identity. But even most cisgender people, if they are truly honest and self-examining, can find ways in which they do not fit within the paradigm for their assigned gender. Explore your own identity, and find the ways in which you may be variant. This will help you to avoid seeing transgender people as "other," which is essential for being an ally.

In an article on the *Pittsburgh Post-Gazette's* website that shares the personal stories of three transgender people, Rayden Sorok, a twenty-seven-year-old transgender man, says,

> One of the biggest changes I've experienced over the past 10 years is I'm continually transitioning. I don't hold myself to rigid standards of what it means to be a man or what it means to be a trans person. I don't think I've crossed over and am on this other side. I think there's this myth that people transition and then they're like another person. We are all changing.

Just as all people are changing and evolving, our laws are evolving, too. As we learn and understand more about ourselves and each other, we work to amend our laws, to bring them closer to truly protecting the life, liberty, and happiness of each individual, regardless of gender, gender expression, race, nationality, sexual orientation, or physical or mental ability. The law has a long way to go in protecting transgender people. We need more specific protections across the board against harassment and discrimination based on gender identity, the same way that we have them for race, sex, nationality, and in many cases, sexual orientation. We need to ensure that transgender people, particularly transgender women of color, no longer die because of violence and ignorance. We need to make prisons safer for transgender people, and end harassment and violence toward transgender people at the hands of law enforcement officials. We need to keep finding ways to make our current laws protect transgender people, and keep fighting to get laws on the books that take those protections to the next level. Only then will we create a society in which every person, no matter their gender identity, is able to express themselves freely and live their own truth.

GLOSSARY

BINARY Something that is composed of two distinct parts.

CATALYST Something that sparks or stimulates a movement, conversation, or event.

CISGENDER An adjective describing someone who identifies with the gender they were assigned at birth.

CORRELATION A particular, defined relationship between things that happen or occur together.

CROSS-DRESSER A person who dresses part of the time, either publicly or privately, in clothing and accessories culturally associated with another gender but does not want to transition to live that way full-time.

DELEGITIMIZE To destroy the credibility of; to make invalid or unworthy of trust.

DRAG KING/QUEEN Someone who dresses in clothing associated with another gender for the sake of performing.

FTM A person who was assigned female at birth but identifies as male; an abbreviation for "female-to-male."

GENDER NONCONFORMING An adjective describing anyone who does not conform or subscribe to traditional ideas of gender and gender expression.

GENDERQUEER An adjective for someone who identifies as being somewhere along the gender spectrum between male and female.

HATE CRIME A violent crime that is motivated by bias against a particular group.

INTERSEX An adjective used to describe someone who was born with physical, hormonal, and/or genetic characteristics associated with both genders.

INTRICACIES Small details.

MTF A person who was assigned male at birth but identifies as female; an abbreviation for "male-to-female."

PARODIED Imitated in a way that is meant to be amusing.

PREFIX A group of letters that comes at the beginning of a word and changes its meaning.

PREVALENCE The condition of being widespread.

PROHIBIT To forbid an action by policy, law, or authority.

TRANSGENDER An adjective describing someone who identifies as a gender other than the one they were assigned at birth.

TRANSSEXUAL An adjective describing someone who has had or is planning to have gender affirmation surgery or hormone therapy.

FOR MORE INFORMATION

Canadian Professional Association for Transgender Health (CPATH)
201-1770 Fort Street
Victoria, BC, Canada, V8R 1J5
Phone: 250-592-6183
Website: http://www.cpath.ca

Founded in 2007 by members of the medical community, CPATH is a professional association of people from many different disciplines who work together for the dignity, health, and well-being of transgender and gender diverse people. They enact this mission through educating professionals, building networks, and advocating for institutional and legislative change.

National Center for Transgender Equality (NCTE)
1400 16th Street NW
Suite 510
Washington, DC 20036
Phone: (202) 642-4542
Email: ncte@transequality.org
Website: http://www.transequality.org

In 2003, the NCTE was founded by transgender activists who saw an urgent need for change to legal policies affecting transgender people. Currently, the center works at the local, state, and federal level to change society through laws and policies. Their mission is to end discrimination and violence against transgender people.

PFLAG Canada
331 Cooper Street, Suite 200
Ottawa, ON, Canada, K2P 0G5
Phone: (888) 530-6777
Email: inquiries@pflagcanada.ca
Website: http://www.pflagcanada.ca
PFLAG Canada is the country's only national organization
   dedicated to helping gay, lesbian, bisexual, transgender,
   transsexual, intersex, and queer Canadians by providing
   support, education, and resources to them and their allies.
   PFLAG, previously known as Parents, Families and Friends of
   Lesbians and Gays, began in 1972 in New York, but has
   developed into an important social force in Canada as well.

Safe Schools Coalition
c/o Equal Rights Washington
PO Box 2388 Seattle, WA 98111
Crisis Hotline: 1-877-SAFE-SAFE (1-877-723-3723)
Message Phone: 206-451-SAFE (7233)
Website: http://www.safeschoolscoalition.org
The Safe Schools Coalition works to make schools safe for LGBT
   students and teachers. The organization provides a wealth of
   resources for transgender and gender nonconforming youth,
   parents/guardians, family members, educators, and allies.

Sylvia Rivera Law Project (SRLP)
147 W 24th Street, 5th Floor
New York, NY 10011
Phone: 212-337-8550
Website: http://srlp.org

Named for transgender activist Sylvia Rivera, who fought against the marginalization of people of color, low-income, and transgender people in the gay rights movement, the SRLP was founded in 2002. The organization believes that the fight for free gender expression for transgender and gender nonconforming people is tied to the fight for social, economic, and racial justice. The SRLP works to increase access to health, legal, and social services for people of color who are transgender, intersex, or gender nonconforming.

Transgender Defense and Legal Education Fund (TDLEF)
20 West 20th Street, Suite 705
New York, New York 10011
Phone: (646) 862-9396
Email: info@transgenderlegal.org
Website: http://tldef.org

Through direct legal services, test-case litigation, public education, public-policy efforts, and community organizing, TDLEF seeks to end discrimination based on gender identity and expression. One of their many programs is the Name Change Project, which connects transgender people with law firms that will provide free legal name-change services.

Transgender Law Center
1629 Telegraph Avenue, Suite 400
Oakland, CA 94612
Phone: (415) 865-0176
Email: info@transgenderlawcenter.org
Website: http://transgenderlawcenter.org

Transgender Law Center believes strongly in the right for people to self-determine their gender identity and expression. The center works to change laws, attitudes, and policies that affect transgender people and all people who do not conform to the gender binary. They work to end the abuse and mistreatment of transgender and gender nonconforming people in prisons, detention centers, and at the hands of law enforcement, and they maintain a network of attorneys who can assist with cases.

WEBSITES

Because of the changing nature of internet links, Rosen Publishing has developed an online list of websites related to the subject of this book. This site is updated regularly. Please use this link to access this list:

http://www.rosenlinks.com/TL/rights

FOR FURTHER READING

Andrews, Arin. Some Assembly *Required: The Not-So-Secret Life of a Transgender Teen.* New York, NY: Simon & Schuster, 2015.

Binnie, Imogen. *Nevada.* New York, NY: Topside Press, 2013.

Bornstein, Kate. *Gender Outlaws: The Next Generation.* Berkeley, CA: Seal Press, 2010.

Boylan, Jennifer Finney. *She's Not There: A Life in Two Genders.* New York, NY: Broadway Press, 2013.

Erickson-Schroth, Laura. *Trans Bodies, Trans Selves.* New York, NY: Oxford, 2014.

Hill, Katie Rain. *Rethinking Normal: A Memoir in Transition.* New York, NY: Simon & Schuster, 2015.

Howell, Ally Winter. *Transgender Persons and the Law.* Chicago, IL: American Bar Association, 2014.

Killermann, Sam. *The Social Justice Advocate's Handbook: A Guide to Gender.* Iowa City, IA: Impetus Books, 2013.

Kuklin, Susan. Beyond Magenta: *Transgender Teens Speak Out.* Somerville, MA: Candlewick, 2015.

Serano, Julia. *Excluded: Making Feminist and Queer Movements More Inclusive.* Berkeley, CA: Seal Press, 2013.

Taylor, Jami Kathleen. *Transgender Rights and Politics: Groups, Issue Framing, and Policy Adoption.* Ann Arbor, MI: University of Michigan Press, 2014.

Teich, Nicholas M. *Transgender 101: A Simple Guide to a Complex Issue.* Berkeley, CA: Cleis Press, 2012.

BIBLIOGRAPHY

Abeni, Cleis. "Mo. Trans Student's Bathroom Struggle is History Repeating Itself." *Advocate*, September 2, 2015. (http://www.advocate.com/transgender/2015/09/02/missouri-trans-students-bathroom-struggle-history-repeating-itself).

Abeni, Cleis. "25 Transgender Pioneers Who Took Us Past the Tipping Point." *Advocate*, December 21, 2015. (http://www.advocate.com/transgender/2015/12/31/25-trans-pioneers-who-took-us-past-tipping-point-2015).

American Civil Liberties Union. "Know Your Rights: Transgender People and the Law." Retrieved April 7, 2016 (https://www.aclu.org/know-your-rights/transgender-people-and-law).

Bush, Katrina. "March and Rally For Baltimore Trans Uprising." ABC, July 4, 2015. (http://www.abc2news.com/news/region/baltimore-city/march-and-rally-for-baltimore-trans-uprising).

Fuoco, Michael. "Three Individuals Share Their Personal Journey Of Transition." *Pittsburgh Post-Gazette*, June 1, 2014. (http://www.post-gazette.com/life/2014/06/01/3-Pittsburgh-transgender-people-share-their-journey-of-discovery-and-transition/stories/201406010205).

GLAAD. "Media Reference Guide- Transgender issues." Retrieved March 4, 2016 (http://www.glaad.org/reference/transgender).

GLAAD. "Tips for Allies of Transgender People." Retrieved March 4, 2016 (http://www.glaad.org/transgender/allies).

Griffin, Pat. "Developing Policies For Transgender Students on High School Teams." National Federation of State High School Associations, September 8, 2015. (https://www.nfhs.

org/articles/developing-policies-for-transgender-students-on-high-school-teams).

Koyama, Emi. "Frequently Asked Questions on Michigan/Trans Controversy." Retrieved April 4, 2016 (http://eminism.org/michigan/faq).

Lambda Legal. "Transgender Rights Toolkit: Fighting Anti-Trans Violence." Retrieved April 9, 2016 (http://www.lambdalegal.org/sites/default/files/publications/downloads/2015_fighting-anti-trans-violence-fs-v7.pdf).

Laverne Cox.com. "Laverne Cox Bio." Retrieved April 7, 2016 (http://www.lavernecox.com/bio-2).

Lesbian, Gay, Bisexual and Transgender Rights Committee. "Know Your Rights: A Guide to Healthcare Rights for Transgender New Yorkers." New York City Bar Association, June2015(http://www2.nycbar.org/pdf/report/uploads/20072875-LGBT-TransgenderRightsBrochureWCover.pdf).

National Center for Transgender Equality. "Know Your Rights: Healthcare." Retrieved March 4, 2016 (http://www.transequality.org/know-your-rights/healthcare).

New York Times Editorial Board. "Prisons and Jails Put Transgender Inmates at Risk." *New York Times*, November 9, 2015. (http://www.nytimes.com/2015/11/09/opinion/prisons-and-jails-put-transgender-inmates-at-risk.html).

Oliven, John F. *Sexual Hygiene and Pathology*, 2nd ed. Philadelphia, PA: JB Lippincott Co, 1965.

Pareene, Alex. "Why the T in LGBT is here to stay – LGBT." *Salon*. October 11, 2007 (http://www.salon.com/2007/10/11/transgender_2).

Stryker, Susan. "Transgender Activism." glbtq. Retrieved March 16, 2016 (http://www.glbtqarchive.com/ssh/transgender_activism_S.pdf).

Time. "25 Transgender People Who Influenced American Culture." May 29, 2014 (http://time.com/130734/transgender-celebrities-actors-athletes-in-america).

Trans Student Educational Resources. "Transgender Day of Visibility." Retrieved May 25, 2016 (http://www.transstudent.org/tdov).

INDEX

ABOUT THE AUTHOR

Rebecca T. Klein has written several young adult books for Rosen over the years. She holds a BA in English from Marygrove College and an MA in English Education from Brooklyn College. She currently lives in Detroit, Michigan, where she teaches middle school English and social studies. She believes strongly in social justice causes, in challenging traditionally held views about gender, and in each individual's right to authentic self-expression.

PHOTO CREDITS